Quelle Histoire
EDITIONS

Graphics: Quelle Histoire
Illustrations: Bruno Wennagel
Text: Albin Quéru and Romain Jubert

Registered office: 3, rue de Paris 75006 Fürstemberg
Editing and design: 80, rue des Haies 75020 Paris

www.quellehistoire.com
contact@quellehistoire.fr

Manufactured by Labelfab/ Printed in France by Stin Imprimerie - Toulouse

PEFC™ 10-31-2841/ **PEFC recycled**/ This product is made from recycled and controlled sources. / pefc-france.org

Francis I

A Vigorous Young Man

You will have a son and this son will be king. It was with these words that a seer is said to have predicted to Louise of Savoy the royal destiny of her son. Francis grew up in the Chateau of Amboise where he developed a passion for archery, tournaments devoted to chivalry and hunting. On January 1, 1515, the king of France, Louis XII, died without leaving a son. So Francis, being the closest cousin, was crowned king of France. The prediction of the seer came to pass and the ambitious young man could finally put his amazing energy to work for the kingdom.

1515

Europe Divided

During this time, three powerful monarchs reigned over Europe. The kingdom of England was ruled by Henry VIII, a hot-tempered and unpredictable sovereign. The Habsburg Empire was governed by the emperor Charles V, a gifted politician who dreamed of a Christian empire that would unite all of Europe! Meanwhile, the newly-crowned Francis I wanted to pursue the conquests of Italy that had been started by the previous kings of France. His first objective was to conquer the duchy of Milan in northern Italy.

1515

Henry VIII
Charles V
Francis I

The Battle of Marignano

Just a few months after his coronation, Francis I crossed the Alps, leading an army of over 30,000 men. Fighting against him were Swiss mercenaries – formidable soldiers reputed to be invincible. The Swiss put everything into place to defend the duchy of Milan, but on September 14, 1515, in Marignan, the bravery of the French combined with their powerful artillery enabled them to defeat the Swiss. It was a blazing success for the young king and for the first time the use of cannon fire made a difference and enabled victory. On the battlefield, Bayard, the «knight without fear and without reproach» congratulated and knighted Francis I!

1515

Da Vinci at the French Court

Even though Francis I was a warrior king, he was also a great supporter of the arts and literature. A keen admirer of the Italian artist Leonardo da Vinci, he invited him to Amboise. The two men got along perfectly to such an extent that Francis I called Leonardo «my father». The painter, seduced by the French court, decided to spend the rest of his life on the peaceful shores of the Loire River. When the artist died on May 2, 1519, the king of France was deeply distressed. He had lost a great artist, but also a faithful friend. It was because of this special relationship between the two men that France has the good fortune to be in possession of the Mona Lisa to this day.

1516

The Concordat

Since the beginning of the 15th century in France, the Roman Catholic Church had been invested with a high degree of autonomy. An electoral system enabled the priests to elect the bishops. In 1516, Francis I decided to put an end to this privilege. He wanted to designate the leaders of the Church of France himself. The Parliament of Paris found this decision to be unjust and refused to give its consent. The king was furious, and compelled Parliament to validate his decision. By imposing his will by force, Francis I intended to impose his authority throughout the entire kingdom.

1516

The Art of Diplomacy

Surrounded by his two rivals, Henry VIII and Charles V, Francis I attempted several times to establish alliances with these monarchs. These encounters offered the occasion for sumptuous feasts during which the king of France put everything into place to impress his guests. In 1520, to welcome Henry VIII, Francis I had immense gold tents erected lined with blue velvet. Unfortunately these attempts turned out to be costly and often fruitless. The very strong personalities of the three men prevented them from reaching agreement.

1520

Pavie

Determined to extend his power into Italy and to compete with the influence of his rival, Charles V, Francis I laid siege to the city of Pavia. On February 24, 1525, the king attacked, forcing the troops of Charles V to retreat. Intrepid and filled with enthusiasm, Francis I pursued his enemies, but the rest of the French army couldn't keep up with him and the king of France found himself surrounded. Forced to surrender, he was taken to Madrid where he was imprisoned. To obtain his freedom, Francis I was forced to give the French province of Burgundy to Charles V.

1525

New France

Christopher Columbus set foot in America in 1492, and from that time on, the great European monarchs multiplied their expeditions to capture this new continent's wealth. In 1534, Francis I sent Jacques Cartier to North America in order to obtain new territories for the kingdom of France. The courageous explorer sailed up the Saint Lawrence River and encountered the Micmac Indians with whom he established friendly relations. These lands would become New France and give rise, many years later, to Canada and Quebec. The navigator undertook two more journeys and brought back the Indian chief Donnacona to the Old World, to introduce him to the king.

1534

The Chateau of Chambord

Francis I enjoyed visiting various places in his kingdom, followed by his entire court, his secretaries, his advisors, his musicians, his chefs...but it was on the banks of the Loire that he most enjoyed hunting and relaxing. In 1519, the king of France chose Chambord to have one of the most beautiful castles of the Renaissance built. The building rises up, majestically, in the middle of an immense hunting domain. A façade of 156 metres, as well as 426 rooms, 77 stairways, 282 fireplaces and 800 sculpted capitals make this unique architectural work one of the crown jewels of Europe.

1536

The Mark of a Great King

For over 30 years, Francis I reigned with authority over the kingdom of France. The «father of the arts and sciences» as his subjects liked to call him put into place numerous ordinances to modernise the kingdom. He made French the official language, created the civil registry and limited the powers of the Church. He was only 53 years old in 1547 when fever overcame him. Aware that he was growing physically weaker, he gave his final recommendations to his son, the future Henry II. His successors would have a hard time ahead of them: soon the wars of religion would disturb the peace of the most powerful kingdom in Europe.

1547

1490

1492
Columbus discovers America

1494
Birth of Francis I

1500
Outbreak of the plague

1515
Coronation of Francis I

1515
Victory in the Battle of Marignano

1516
Arrival of da Vinci in Amboise

1517
Beginning of the Reformation

1519
Construction of the Chateau de Chambord

1519
Death of Leonardo da Vinci

1525
Defeat [illegible] the Batt[illegible] of Pavi[illegible]

1528
Construction of the castle of Fontainebleau

1534
Arrival of Jacques Cartier in Canada

1542
Creation of the Inquisition tribunal

1555
Nostradamus' *Centuries astrologiques*

1560

1526
Treaty of
drid; release
f Francis I

1532
Union of Brittany and France

1539
French becomes official language of the kingdom

1547
Death of Francis I

1559
Death of Henry II

Europe in the 16th century
1
2
3
4
5
6

Key to the MAP

1 The Battle of Marignano

In 1515, having been king for just a few months, Francis I won a decisive victory at Marignano in northern Italy. All of Europe was impressed!

2 The House of Tudor

Of Welsh origin, the Tudors ruled England from 1485 to 1603. Following the War of the Roses, this powerful family imposed itself on the throne.

3 The House of Habsburg

This was a royal family that ruled the Holy Roman Empire from 1452 to 1740. This empire included, in particular, southern Italy, Spain and Austria.

4 The Field of the Cloth of Gold

In 1520 Francis I invited Henry VIII to France to negotiate a peace treaty. He had a magnificent camp built to impress his guest.

5 Union of Brittany and France

By marrying Anne of Brittany's daughter, then signing the edict of union August 13, 1532, Francis I definitively united Brittany and the kingdom of France.

6 The chateaux of the Loire

The chateaux of the Loire date from the 11th century, but it was the Renaissance period in which jewels such as Chenonceau, Clos Lucé and especially Chambord saw the light of day.

Kingdom of France

Francis I's conquests

The Holy Roman Empire

Kingdom of England

Ottoman Empire

Portraits

Henry VIII

(1491-1547)

King of England from 1509 to 1547, Henry VIII was a very strong personality! First an ally, then an enemy of Francis I, he went down in history for having six different wives, which angered the Pope and forced Henry to separate from the Roman Church.

Charles V

(1500-1558)

Heir to the duchy of Burgundy, Charles eventually led the Holy Roman Empire. A great rival of Francis I, he captured the latter in Pavia and demanded a very large ransom for the king of France.

Leonardo da Vinci

(1452-1519)

A brilliant artist, painter, sculptor and inventor, Leonardo da Vinci was one of the brightest stars of the Renaissance. Born in Italy, da Vinci was invited by Francis I to come to France in 1516. The artist spent the rest of his life on the peaceful banks of the Loire.

Jacques Cartier

(1491-1557)

Born in Saint-Malo, Jacques Cartier was a 16th-century French navigator. In 1534, with the support of Francis I, he embarked on his first expedition to North America. It led to the French settling in the beautiful region that would become Quebec.

Game

IMAGE HUNT

Hunt for these pictures in the scene on the right:

Francis I

The tobogganist

Charles V

Louis XII

The intruder

The cook

Jacques Cartier

Leonardo da Vinci

Henry VIII

The sleeper

The dog

Martin Luther

The swimmer

The hunter

The carpenter

Rabelais

The perching man

Charles of Bourbon

The climber

The priest

Game

7 DIFFERENCES

Find the 7 differences between the left-hand and right-hand pictures

Solution: bird, cloud, cheek, mountain; horse's tail; horse's hoof; dog's ears

Game

MAZE

Help Francis I to find his salamander

Game

SILHOUETTES

Which one is Francis I's silhouette?

Correct answer: silhouette a

Game

QUIZ

1. Which famous battle did Francis I win on September 14, 1515?

a. Waterloo
b. Poitiers
c. Marignano
d. Bouvines

2. What chateau was built in 1519 on the orders of Francis I?

a. The Louvre
b. Chambord
c. Versailles
d. Vincennes

3. Which artist moved to Château d'Amboise at the request of Francis I?

a. Michelangelo
b. Sandro Botticelli
c. Raphael
d. Leonardo da Vinci

Correct answers: 1.c / 2.b / 3.d

Discover

the Quelle Histoire apps, too!

A collection of interactive applications to learn about history in a fun way!

For more information visit: www.quellehistoire.org